Cutlery Bugs

Entomologist Emma

BookLeaf
Publishing
India | USA | UK

Presentation by *BookLeaf Publishing*

Web: www.bookleafpub.com

E-mail: info@bookleafpub.com

ISBN: 9789357446457

First edition 2022

Harry the Tarantula

Harry the tarantula,
Was a fuzzy old beast.
He loved to go tapdancing,
And enjoy yummy fly feasts.

He danced everyday,
And never made webs.
He made quite a clang,
As he had spoons for his legs.

Sally the Ladybird

Sally the cheerleader,
Was a small ladybird.
She'd flip in the air,
Like a red fuzzy blur.

Her pom poms were purple,
And her uniform blue.
She had egg beaters for wings,
And legs made of corkscrews.

Ed the Grasshopper

Ed the grasshopper,
Was a skateboarding pro.
He'd do awesome kickflips,
And could put on a show.

He knew every trick,
And was a gold medal skater.
But Ed's a little bit odd,
As he's made from a cheese grater.

Tily the Bull-Ant

Tily the bull ant,
Was a keen dressmaker.
She'd sew fashion lines,
And lived in a salt shaker.

With tongs for pincers,
She could sew any stitch.
Threading a needle,
Never caused any hitch.

Bob the Dung Beetle

Bob the dung beetle,
Loved flying a kite.
And dreamed he could soar,
To such dizzying heights.

So, he fashioned some wings,
From a rusty coke can.
And made a propeller,
with an old oven fan.

Fae the Butterfly

6

This ice-cream taster,
Was a blue butterfly.
She called herself Fae,
And had saucepans for eyes.

She loved peanut butter,
And adored cookie dough.
But her best ice-cream flavour,
Was stinky troll toes.

Bertikins the Flea

Bertikins the flea,
Was an artistic painter.
He loved goji berries,
And lived in a tea strainer.

He wore an old pot,
As a fashionable hat.
And painted with beetroot,
With sploshes and splats.

Maggie the Weevil

Maggie the weevil,
Was a pro acrobat.
She rode a unicycle,
And wore ramekin hats.

She juggled eight melons,
With her rolling pin snout.
And lived in a rice cooker,
Which was very burnt out.

Curtis the Snail

Curtis the snail,
Tried hopscotch one day.
But a snail can't hop,
In any such way.

He put a spring whisk,
On the top of his shell.
And hopped upside down,
Until he felt really unwell.

Milly the Stick Bug

Milly the stick bug,
Loved to hula hoop.
She's made from a soup ladle,
And a rusty ice-cream scoop.

She'd twist and she'd turn,
Those six egg rings around,
They'd spin faster and faster,
And never fall down.

Leo the Cricket

Leo the cricket,
Was part of a band.
With cake beaters for legs,
He played drums for the fans.

They partied all night,
Making quite a loud din.
And played heavy metal,
On silver cake tins.

Ava the Cockroach

Ava the cockroach,
Lived in a bread bin.
She loved to go bowling,
Knocking down pins.

She often hit strikes,
And was a top scorer.
She's made from tea spoons,
And an old apple corer.

Gary the Mozzie

Gary the Mozzie,
Lived in an old shoe.
He spent his days knitting,
And slurping lamb stew.

He had skewers for legs,
And he used them to knit.
He made lots of socks,
With a clickety click.

Paige the Fly

Paige the scuba diver,
Was a noisy black fly.
She'd explore ocean caves,
With salt shaker eyes.

She'd plunge to great depths,
Down where it was dark.
She loved ocean critters,
But not tiger sharks.

Ned the Daddy Long Legs

Ned the daddy long legs,
Was a wannabe whiz.
He played the piano,
And worked in show biz.

He could play the chopsticks,
As he had them for feet.
But he can't hold a note,
Or keep a good beat.

Vicki the Mantis

16

Vicki the mantis,
Was a pro weightlifter.
She could raise 3 kilos,
In a red flour sifter.

She was a tough bug,
And had metal feelers.
She was made of strong steel,
From large veggie peelers.

Ernie the Centipede

Ernie the grump,
Was an old centipede.
He played table tennis,
And munched pumpkin seeds.

He could hit every serve,
And play all night long.
He had spatula legs,
Which were great for ping pong.

Sootie the Bee

Sootie the bee,
Is a true golfing nut.
She's made from a kettle,
And loves mini putt putt.

She will whack golf balls,
Up and down the green.
She has cookie cutters wings,
And guzzles caffeine.

Arty the Wasp

Arty the wasp,
Was a cool DJ.
He rocked a cake turntable,
Mixing music to play.

He could rock any tune,
And was made from a whisk.
The party was pumping,
When he played disc after disc.

Marissa the Termite

Marissa the termite,
Was an Olympic athlete.
She loved figure skating,
And had cheese knives for feet.

She would jump in the air,
And easily rotate.
She would dance with such grace,
As she'd skate and she'd skate.

George the Leafhopper

George the leafhopper,
Was in a tough race.
He rode BMX bikes,
Always winning first place.

He was made from a zester,
And was difficult to catch.
He would leap over the jumps,
His foes were no match.